DAMMTOR

DAMMTOR

James Sheard

CAPE POETRY

Published by Jonathan Cape 2010

2 4 6 8 10 9 7 5 3 1

Copyright © James Sheard 2010

James Sheard has asserted his right under the Copyright, Designs
and Patents Act 1988 to be identified as the author of this work

First published in Great Britain in 2010 by
Jonathan Cape
Random House, 20 Vauxhall Bridge Road,
London SW1V 2SA

www.rbooks.co.uk

Addresses for companies within The Random House Group Limited can be found at:
www.randomhouse.co.uk/offices.htm

The Random House Group Limited Reg. No. 954009

A CIP catalogue record for this book
is available from the British Library

ISBN 9780224090735

The Random House Group Limited supports The Forest Stewardship Council (FSC),
the leading international forest certification organisation. All our titles that are
printed on Greenpeace approved FSC certified paper carry the FSC logo.
Our paper procurement policy can be found at:
www.rbooks.co.uk/environment

Typeset in Bembo by Palimpsest Book Production Limited,
Grangemouth, Stirlingshire
Printed and bound in Great Britain by
MPG Books, Bodmin, Cornwall

In memory of my father, Michael Sheard, 1933–2008

What travesty is it then that they enact in the cave with veiled faces? For they cover their eyes lest their deeds of shame should revolt them. Some like birds flap their wings imitating the raven's cry; others roar like lions ... what shameful mockeries for men who call themselves wise.
Ambrosiaster

Self-sacrifice is voluntary and involuntary at the same time.
Jung

CONTENTS

DAMMTOR

A LIST OF NECESSARY ITEMS

for Tony Williams

Someone else's Poetic Licence.

Your editor's signature in the form of a rubber stamp.

Cordite ink.

Wire, matches, terminals.

Three keys:
to the Helsinki safehouse;
to the Scunthorpe *pied-à-terre*;
to the lock she changed.

A miniature cassette you have never listened to.

A transcript of every sigh she made.

As a memento of that last Baltic holiday, a polished shell
    (.303 caliber).

A blurry foetal scan from the abandoned Homo Poeticus project.

An air-brush.

A first draft of your rival's most famous poem, folded into a paper
    tiger.

A denunciation, complete except for the name.

A jade snuff bottle.

A blend of Gawith's No. 8 and the powdered bones of his hand.

KNIFE

Once,
I remember –
although not clearly
for I am dull now and held
in a broken clasp of tortoiseshell,
in the loose grip of a soft hand –
but once, as I say, you were
my whetstone, slick
and spat-upon.

DAMMTOR

It's May,
you thought,
and after rain.
White hawthorn
had taken the tracksides,
and no matter where we dig,
you thought,
we find a tilted land
on a tipped earth.

It's soft,
you thought,
the long grey scar
of vanished rails.
Something in your pack
sounded like hoofbeats.
Poor luggage lay piled
on the gravel. You thought

of how Dammtor
was a station for midnights,
hitched up on stone legs,
hollow with sunken light,
with the swallowed plosives
of church-space. You thought

of places to be broke in,
too late to go home from.
Places to watch
a welder in the high girders.
His flaring iris hissing shut.
Yours stuck open.

THE TRANSLATOR

Some people imagine that I find her
creamy and clear-skinned upon her pages.
That she arranges herself for me just so.
That I can gather her up and place her
where she needs to be.

But she lies in a language, and language lies
in a wrecking-yard. I stalk and haunt
its strange symmetries, its twisted piles,
its interlocks and parabolas.
I tug out her severed foot, her three fingers.
I look for her torso.
I need false plates
for my fridge-truck.

Sometimes, and late, I call her.
And if my mouth is moved to speak,
it says this:

Let us buy bread and wine.
Let your bread be my bread.
Let your wine be my wine.
Let us place them in a bag
which is both your bag and mine.
Let us carry them to a home
which is a home I know.
Let your table
be my table.
Let your people
be mine.

They are the worst dreams she wrote
because they are the dreams
in which I am happy.

I know them.
I know how you wake
to dust on the water
and a stone in your head.

I know how we dream
that the rooms are white
and the ceilings high,
and we float, untethered
towards one another.

But then, I thought,
so do the drowned
in their slow tumbling
through the churn of the world.
Eyes open. Hands resting
as if on a velvet cushion.

Two shut doors she wrote
across an unswept landing.
Where we might tread water
in our separate pools.

IN THE ATTIC

I.

Before waking,
having slept with new images of you,
I traced each detail of a peculiar blackness:
The wing-shadow of a bird too far out
to ever dip landwards,
the somehow-darkness
of snow at sea.

And so,
our images being what we sometimes are,
and despite my waking to find my skin
once more among the sunlit –
this is the poem that rafts me into morning,
you the dark island I fetch up against.

II.

Something, you said, *should burn here.*
But nothing burnt there
in the nothing-burns-here wind. Then,

beneath your hands,
rose a sudden Chinese-fan-edge of fire.
It moved ghostly, upwards,
its shape random,
then gone.

You lowered your eyes. I said
*Let me be the ghost
in your burning building.*

III.

You spoke of startled uprides,
of waking to me beside you.

You called me *Animal*
of Many Kills, stood moonlit
in cold clouds of your hair.

You said
Skinful of Nothing,
the slow blood streams
like hair against my neck.

Then you uncoiled,
and flew open into madness,
into a flaring fall of stars.

WAS

It was in the low-slung sun.
It was in the hum of arousal.
It was in the leaf pressed up
to our casement window.
It was in the way
that light lay broken.
It was the blotting-out
of the world beyond.

It was in the leaf
and its crablike shadow
which spread its fingers
across your face.
It was in the leaf's hand
which drove your head
down and down
into the downy pillow.

It was in that sense
of being slack and taut,
like bent wire stretched
between broken poles.
It was in a future,
and that, in turn,
was a road blackened
by recent rain.

It was in the cramp.
It was in the rictus.
It was in the crippling
of hand and eye.
It was in how we rose
without ascension
to other business,
the mere use of time.

VERTIGO

Consider how, between that word and this,
some beast might lift a wary head,
its yellowed tusks curled upwards in enquiry.

His mood might flash through forest light,
make shadows switch on barks of trees
that now reclaim every inch of ground you've cleared.

And all that time you've palmed from left to right
recoils with a snap. Your fingers clutch.
Your throat seals shut.

Then mountains lift and liquefy, seas curdle into rock,
stars tear clear of looping roots of mass and light
and boil away, between that word and this.

AUBADE

Of the nine concrete blocks
set before the station,
I choose the third.
It was meant for my monument.

Last night, all night, the night
streamed from me.
I shed ashes and silver.
My skin remade itself. My pupils
flared and narrowed
in the shifting lights.

I found you, love, coiled
around a bar-stool and abandonment.
Your mouth made *moues*
of various kinds. For all that,
I heard only: *Hate me.*
Hate me.

So, by degrees,
I brought you slowly home.
Now you, too, are neatly stacked
among the other logs
in the special place

as behind me, someone scratches
the concourse with his brush.
I too have things to clean
and a path to trace.

But for now, I slow,
grow almost still, then
drop into this pocket
the morning has made for me.

TAKEN

When I was taken to the place
where the others were taken,
it felt as though I was rendered
into circles. My skin scraped
like gritty stone, then slackened.
The tunnel dog-legged into light.

The one who took me forced my head
to look into the pool of myself.
I was shown a tree where I might hang.
I was hanged from it.

This thing broke, then that.
I took comfort from the wet
to which I was returning,
from the springy crush of moss beneath me.
Light tangled around me, then we fell together
like a stillness.

And if I am still here,
it is in the sense of October sunlight.
I am here, then not here, then here again.
If I am here, where I was taken,
I am moments of light
on an empty ground.

THE STRANDPERLE NOTEBOOK

But a voice that scorns chorales is yelling 'Wanker!'
                    Tony Harrison, *V.*

1.

There's oil and backwash from these boats
departing Hamburg's morning wharves.
There's stalking cranes. Men pull and tote.
One street back the sleepy whores
lean out from clubs. They clutch their towels.
They call for milk and fresh-bagged rolls,
their wigs in sun like lacquered cowls
as Hamburg's one-note church bells toll.

2.

Fat Helmie at his fresh fish stall
slaps flat ice with a varnished plank.
He lays out cod in muscled rows,
then sweeps a wash of crushed ice back.
It crisps the scales. It makes the eyestones
catch the light. His own are dull
with thirty years of beer and schnapps.
He sniffs and grunts. He curses gulls
which Stuka-bomb his grubby cap.

3.

I'll drink this cup then wander out
on lazy feet to seek Strandperle –
that slice of sand on which you'd lounge
and watch the ferries pass the markers
draining boats onto this land.
I never could afford a cabin.
I'd come in big-boned, raw and dumb
from two nights pacing decks.

The thing is, darling, what you took
for some mute hunger –
English shy-bloke ways –
was really hope we'd somehow skip
your welcome rites.
I needed sleep.

4.

I'd like to spin this coffee out.
I'd like to work a longer line.
I'd like to pull my punch and let my mouth
sip a little longer at the scene, take time
to summon shapes from Hamburg's autumn air
and taste the coalbrick smoke from tiled stoves
which squat fat-legged in Hamburg's flats.
From here,
the view past Helmie's stall moves on,
above the ferry-landing's
greying concrete domes
to where the Elbridge lifts, dips, lifts –
it spans poor homes and drydocks
with its spinal curvature.

5.

You claimed I learnt to write in Hamburg.
All our fracture tore love's borders ragged,
tore my even surface loose and cold.
I came to think that poems were stages
stripped of sets. Their rotten floors
should give out at unwary pressure
to oubliettes of metaphor.
But, perhaps, a poem's a well-worked tract
nailed up on greyed oak doors,
and what we think of is less the scrap of paper –
more the scutcheoned locks,

the brasswork,
the grim gargoyled arch,
the buttressed stonework,
spaces, speech.
That sense of crypts
beneath our feet.

6.

He Luchts wear oilwaxed Heinrich caps
to lie straight-faced. They're paid to make
these Hamburg matrons' shoulders shake
on harbour tours. Fantastic maps of Hamburg's past:

Navvies dug the Elbe out inside a month.
That old-tyre-hung and battered tug
is Sheikh Yamani's yacht. His son's
fourth wife's runabout's that tanker.
Now to your left, the Michelskirche –
that weather-vane weighs sixteen tons.

I muse on how my jowls have thickened:
His weathered face remains the peak
of artwork by a team of craftsmen:
leather-workers, trained on teak.

7.

Other Hamburg occupations:
A barker strains a Russian suit
and growls that girls inside *Show More.*
You wonder what such *More* could mean,
when standing on the Reeperbahn –
these three square miles of anatomy
and cunts spread like dissectagrams.
Chimney-sweeps with costumed shoulders

scuffed where fingers press for luck;
Frumped-down Muttis hissing *Süsse*
out from doorways, warm in comfy
coats and hats – their punters
mainly shy and just-past-school boys
needing someone who won't laugh.

8.

We'd meet at Hase's Bike-Repair-Shop-
And-Marxist-Dialectic-Class,
Drink in *Zum Gipfel* – a secret knock
might get you in. You'd wash a glass
and try the pumps and hope
that mine-host Stephan Leer,
the 'World's First Deaf Anarcho-Landlord',
had finally installed some beer.

9.

And while we may have toppled pylons,
scuppered goods trains, marched and thrown
neat Hamburg cobbles, occupied whole blocks
of houses, what I think of's more the drone
of internecine mock-symposia,
of splinter groups and endless blame;
weekends lost to tossed-back Korn; rows of pills,
and coming down with flash-dried herbage,
grown on chipped-paint windowsills.

10.

Bruises formed by truncheon strikes
are strange. A bar of vivid white
marks out the impact. From the edges
streak out slender chains of bloodburst
scurrying beneath the skin.

Bruising formed by rape:
Blue finger marks. Four punctured prints
along each inner thigh, and there,
offset by just that span
which marks us out from other beasts,
the glorious opposing thumb.
All rendered dark by how light breaks
through that bath you shouldn't take.

Bruises made by bullets: leaking
haematoma, spreading outwards
like a wash of solid yellow-ochre mottling
painted on with broad-edged brush.

Malnutrition bruising: clotted welts,
the blood pushed upwards by the bone
to lump the skin in dark necrotics.
Seen in deserts, prisons, homes.

II.

I've made no move towards Strandperle,
but climbed this nearby mound to view
a weighty statue of Graf Bismarck.
Hitler used this image, too:
a planted sword with hilt at crotch-height,
meek bowed head – a Teuton knight,
but humble, conscious of the weight
of lethal duty.
And lately, politicians at Ground Zero:
unsure men, all looking down
as if checking that their dicks have grown.

That night, I found your bedroom rank
with sweaty hangers-on.
Some would-be lawyer taking photos.
The polaroid's flat cloudy tongue
still toying with your spine and thighs,
that tender join between your breast and side.
Now lift her arm! Your eyes as wide
as coin blanks between the punch and die.

I seem resolved to ditch Strandperle.
To get there now, I'd have to turn
my dogleg verses past this length
of Dock-Front Loft-Life New Conversions,
and think about the night I left.
Whilst I flew, the Wall came down:
Ossis peered through battered nets
of iron twistrods shorn of concrete,
to see some Yuppies clutching Sekt.
The Stasi files spilled outwards from
those close-packed metal shelves. Crumbled
cheap-weave papers loosed some spore
which drifted West and struck us dumb.

And *Selbstkritik*'s a sourish sweet,
sucked in secret, lips curled in.
I pace, without much hope of footprint
along this grey and narrowed fringe
that thinks that irony's a cop-out,
a self-serving way of giving in.
I want a meta-poem, stripped and dull:

'Scene. Polemic. Memorial.'

Fat Helmie clears his stall.
Late morning walkers dodge his spray.
It pushes up the blood-stained ice
to ruffs of tawny cod intestines.
The sound of cups of coffee
clacking down on glass.
And in my mouth
that taste of brass.

TWO ICONS OF ROSA LUXEMBURG

I.

Here's Rosa's face,
it's shaded out
by halo light
and photo crop.

II.

Here's Rosa's face
it's been smeared flat
by rifle butts
and water rot.

Cleanse these tricky instruments of mine,
my hands and tongue.
Use fresh water, then
let them settle, still and pale.
And let me play the sleepy priest
who speaks no word till listening's done.

Yes, cleanse these instruments of mine,
my hands and tongue.
Let me sit as cool and dumb
as three stones on a dusty sill.
Or drift aloft like lazy smoke
seeping from an unwatched hill.

LIGHT, LAKE

I am not a man
for even light.
I like it broken,
my shadow partial.
I like the lit world
seen through lattices,
the sun through rushes,
a lantern set swinging.

Yet I am a man
for the upland lake.
It finds a level
in the broken land.
And, still or ruffled,
it lies there waiting
for my head to lower;
to pause; then drink.

BUSINESS IN HELSINKI

We wear ties as bright
as excise stamps.
Our shoes wax and crackle
like letters of credit.

We lay down our meetings –
thin mortar between
warehouse brickwork,
muting the horns of winter.

The atrium holds light
and harbour cobbling,
track where cranes once shuffled,
sidelong and chafing.

The old scents of value
ghost and curl – roasting, curing,
the sharp musts of hessian,
and fat slabs of fur.

So we trade our poor filaments
of thought and fraudulence,
as Baltic light strikes flat
and the sea curdles into ice,

shape uneasy handshakes
over deals of frail value
amid rumours that – northwards –
the evergreens shatter,

however soft the closing of your fist.

COMPOUND COUNTRY

We're out of season.
The chairs are cleared.
The pool stays flat.
The lobby's dull with uncut wax.
A cane-and-cut-glass chandelier
lies outspread like a polypod.
Our mornings flutter by with books.
The barman makes his brasswork glitter
with vinegar and a twist of cloth.

At night, the headlands push out arms
pricked with beads of coastal lights.
They bleed a little of what lies behind:
the South shines orange; the North glows green.
The night we crossed the plain to here,
the hills tracked us like arcing fins.
The driver nodded to the shattering flares
of some wired compound, turned and grinned:

'Your country! Your country, over there!'

Haloed still, the saints' purged faces
Still raimented, if that's the word
for colours draining down the walls
towards the rubble, weeds and turds.

Map-marked still, the streets you named me.
Yes, still extant, if that's the term
for pockmarked hulks of wired-off houses
where rats and sentries take their turns.

That jetty's there – the one you swam from.
It still strides out, if that's the phrase
for broken pilings stripped of planking
within the watchtower's arc and range.

The hill-road's open. The uplands offer
cool relief, if that's the point
of all this earth-art angled southwards:
flags and slogans. Threats and taunts.

WAITING FOR DISSOLUTION

Fountains, 1539

They say that grey roofleads peeled back
like wet leaves from Rievaulx's rafters.
We loose the rot of our own trapped prayer.
Twitch off sour blankets.
Rise to pre-dawn duties.

This morning,
no workers have come
from the outlying granges.
Perhaps we too will trudge from the valley
to find their plank doors shut tight
beneath keystones of pagan heads.

From the pulpit stair
comes something like the creaking of stirrups.
The reader stands
like an outrider above his saddle.
We think of panels splintering, the grind and
give of a knife,
twisting in the stone lips of a shell.

And from the cupped murmur of the mealtime reading,
we scrape something less than pearls or flesh.
We wait. We watch the flames
beat black bruising on the fireback.

clara considers bells –
not the thick stiff tongues
banging in the shadow of arches
but hard peas dancing
behind silver slitmouths
of one horse pumping
vapours and metal
among proper little trees
in a proper little park
all the way
all the way

I DO NOT SEE THIS PICTURE

We studied it, the sea,
its buckings and outbawlings,
saw how the crooked finger of the headland
looked like an invitation,
how the moonlight was hammered flat
into one long metal road,
how stones were dragged round the coast
to their obliteration.

One of us called
from an unshaped throat.
No consonants ridged us in.
The fingers of another
sketched simple shapes —
ideas, needs,
people scattering.

Was this the sound
of the whole unweighed mass of water,
or its breaking,
its unnumbered fragments?
The sky's storming
was bent in beneath.
The I thundered
in our throats and ears.
We were surf in its moment of light,
arcing backwards.

THE MITHRAS MACHINE

The Grades of Mithras: Raven, Bride, Soldier, Lion, Persian,
Sun-Courier, Father

I.

This lintel is a dark landing of cargo from that bellied perfection of
our fathers around my stab of torchlight something gathers like oil
hungering up the drill   I grow then crack open as false sleep some-
times does to a chemical light on northumberland moors   I spit out
something uneasy this door is the entrance to a mithras cave   here
blood is the point   here hunched men shuffled through the decks
of what they had made   I had wondered what my cupped hands
held mismatched fortunes   perhaps the shape of that slim-laked place
where I grew up   of strange palms pressed to my lovers throat   an
opened mussel picked for luck from endless whitened baltic flats
when mourning you   but mithraic ground is not the sand of cool
ribs under idle lovers feet   its the bulls great heartbeat slamming
shut around the stab of shortened spears the stun of axe-backs wielded
close   how dying beasts will rage and gape their blood like angry
heat comes pouring down on desert floors   soldiers dragged the
mithras bull to here then left its rags of gut and skin to fray in romes
collapse and through a harsh dark flower of britain raising spines
within a slowly closing fist of angles saxons jutes and picts perhaps
they stitched my shoddy cloak of remnant cloth   its true I often
make a move that dips my horns between these shoulders and then
glance up to emphasise a boyish look in knowing eyes and think
such subtle strength will tilt the switch that leaves the womans yes
unsaid but now I know the bull is dead

II.

I played the raven well at least I have been dressed up in oily blacks
with just that touch of colour block the focus that the british lack
she said   I felt I perched against the sun and made a tailored shape
of strength my voice choked up with consonants and brought no

words from gods when asked to augur out the guts men spill and
now for all my strangled noise and articulated questing of my head
I fly nowhere the ravens dead

III.

I stood in thin-soled shoes and felt the stone of church-aisle seep
the cold of waiting up to interleave with doubt   the action lapped
towards my suited back in 2/4 time borne in on whispers and I
hoped the odd lament   the figure broke into my sight a stranger
hair coiled up and rendered tight it seemed with moulds of slow-
dripped lead she wore a mask I wondered when some acolyte would
lean in close to tell me that my bride was dead

IV.

Warrior heres the question will you take this crude-cut stone to
batter in her rapists skull hack his bollocks off and stuff his mouth to
shut that half-heard crowing up do some violence of your own   see
her still there grabbed and torn to silence hunched beneath the
bathroom sink   or would you first require a week in some faked
grove of sweathuts stewing in a wishful alchemy of grunts and farts
and pissing on the bark of trees as if that conjured warlike arts   to
forge a petty iron john from that metal mickey youve become   let
me guess however red your mists of rage your soldiers dead

V.

I said cleanse these tricky instruments of mine my hands and tongue
use honey let them settle still and pale let hcr rail against the metal
screams of apes and let me play the sinless lion priest his utter still-
ness coiled around the roar which comes one day when listenings
done   but think too how my restful golden hands could clutch and
stick of how my sweetened tongue will flicker through its lore of
softened words yet still could rasp its grainy hoard of sugars out
along the line of crawling skin   then perhaps turn once more towards

the leathered clutch of apes intent on doing further harm   no lion
lifts his carved head to roar for though the pale priest lives on the
lions dead

VI.

I played the persian well at least I have been dressed up in costly
greys   heard it supposed I would father well   asked to seed land
not-yet-turned and then too parched   or more often ground too
lushly full of phantom fruit for comfort flashing with a future just
too cute for contemplation   I think of perses flinging gouts of
semen out on earth and stone and then recall it was the bulls and
not his own   such things we hoard or at least release to places
where they cannot snag give me children but not yet until its clear
the persians dead

VII.

Strange how ancients thought the sun a lofted torch a chariot locked
within a curving run or the one I always liked the best a shuffling
beetle shunting dung from east to west so here while your hands
claw at my chest and pupils twitch around my shape I am both
flaming mask and that which masks the sunlight out fingers curl
around my nape but also bring a thumb to press against my throat
I raise a cobra arm as if to strike but then extend one finger out to
curse the father by the bed and wish and wish the sun was dead

VIII.

I have been no father and I was a piss-poor son but still I tend my
backroom mint and strike out coins to the front some petty wisdom
and on the rear my lifted profile stern and just and when you raise
your unsure eyes I set my face to something bland a level gaze with
just a hint of reprimand and yes my chest and arms for comfort
here but remember that my iron-tipped staff has rested on the bloody
glaze of tiled mithraic floors and how I have led the rites that make
the dead

There was a rule
and the rule said
that once was ok
and twice if you had to.
She laid the rule down
on our scarred table,
on our head-stained pillow –
she stirred it into our coffee
with a tarnished spoon.
She laughed, I laughed:
because once *was* ok,
and sometimes you had to
fuck them twice: to tie up
the frayed end;
to slap them down;
for pleasure, for vengeance.
Sometimes you had to,
had to, had to.
So for each one, once –
or twice if I had to –
I would bring strong tea
to her morning room, and kneel
to the slats of her low bed,
to her seaweedy scent,
to his surprise. She grinned,
I grinned. I laid the tray
on her lacquered table
and padded away. Because
once was ok, and twice
if you had to, had to, had to.
As for her, she would sit
in the kitchen's dark, watch
the hallway, listen for my steps

and the steps of the others,
let smoke drift into the light.
She stayed silent. She had to.
She most liked the time when
my soaked sleep was deepest.
She would crouch on my floor,
finger the clothing and whisper.
I would wake, yes, but lie still.
I had to, had to, had to.

THAT LAST DRIVE

Once that last silence
had risen around us
sour roadlights swung
by and
by
like lazy hammers,
striking slatecuts from your face.

LETTERS

Of those last letters that you wrote
I must say I preferred the first –
the one where you were bitter, calm and terse,
the one where you were at my throat.

The second struck a different note –
sloppy, drunk, yet full of thirst
for all those things you'd claimed would hurt
in the first one that you wrote.

BEECHES

Some waists have thickened,
but few grow straight.
Some hold postures,
though it aches
to proffer breasts
and buttocks up.
So pass along
the flint-strewn path
and bow your head
and count to ten,
and when you next
pass beeches, think:
*these are old lovers; this
is how I left them.*

BREAD

My mother's bread
Was a gaping bread
The cut along the dough too deep.
My mother's bread
Was a gaping bread
The plump ends nicked too far.

My mother's bread
was a two toned bread
too pale in the cut, too dark in the crust.
My mother's bread
Was a two toned bread
The crests raised high and dark.

My mother's bread
Was a vanishing bread
It grew stubby as the week went by.
My mother's bread
Was a vanishing bread
It squatted among the hams.

My mother's bread
Is a forgotten bread
No bread, she said, *is hard.*
My mother's bread
Is a forgotten bread
No bread, she said, *is hard.*

THE OSTEOPATH

He somehow keeps his hands
on the cool side of tepid.
The temperature never alters.

His touch on my back
is something less than human,
sharkskin, perhaps, cured and turned

inside out. *These are not gloves*
he tells me. *These are my palms.*
I lie, crouch, kneel. *Fall into me,*

he says, having wrapped me
around a fetal cushion. He holds on
and dances, moving to some rhythm

only he feels within me. And that
is it: it's what he detects inside me,
the levers and pulleys of my frame,

beneath what the years have draped
across me. His fingers hook onto the bone
of a body forgotten, but not quite gone.

ABSURDIST. IRRITANT. FRIEND.

for Martijn Benders

They grow pale and bitter,
the endives of Brabant.
Tubed in cardboard,
they suck up the dark
musts of earthen floors.
Light cannot touch them.

So sweeten them
with gouts of cheesesauce.
Smoke them out
with fattened bacon.
Soften them a little
in an oven set to stun.

Then let them grin upwards
from the delftware,
their sharper teeth filed flat
beneath that bubbled wig.

AMONG THE ANTHOLOGIES

i.m. E.A. Markham 1939–2008

It was heard as if at night, lying slotted
in a tier of bunks, in a rough-washed shelter
taken against a worsening sky. All day,

I had trekked in search of the '*After . . .*' poem,
making steady progress on the rise and fall
of pages flicked from back to front, and passing

waymarker after waymarker, each one waiting
for the day when the passes would be closed
and snow would barrel up and break them.

And because my eyes had been dipped
below the titles, on the sloping line which lies
beneath the poem's horizon, I heard

our newly dead singing to their recent dead,
and the brawling of their young
who now, in turn, sing them
over these unforgiving tops, and down.

THIN

Forgive me, Sir,
I'm writing thin.
The aperture
lets no light in.
No image flips
inside the case,
and no light falls
upon the plate.

Upon the plate,
no light will fall.
Inside the case,
no image flip.
No light gets in
the aperture.
I'm writing thin –
Forgive me, Sir.

AFTER THE FUNERAL

The bird had nothing to add.
It dippered the churned gravel
from a lip of corroded stone.

The hour, the day had been blown
by a glassblower. The bird
made the light all wrong,

but watched by gate and kerb
as we pawed the tarmac, swollen
and shining. We shook hands.

The bird stooped low, rose fast,
came to a sudden stop
on a crumbled wing.

It shuffled sideways, making room.
No companion came.

WITHIN DAYS

In those months, my dreams took on
the wit and pomp of prophecy.
A child was lifted from a burning book,
Our Lady of Freiburg melted, then ran red
through the lanes and gutters of evening.
And when I woke, it was to the slatted light
found only in poems.
To a domed belly beside me,
the snorks and snuffles of the host.

★

Within days, my dreams took on
the blood and smoke of prophecy.
A child was lifted from a roadside brook,
our bones melted and we ran mad
through each flare and guttering of morning.
And when I woke, it was to the slatted light
found only in poems.
To the even breath beside me,
the snorks and snuffles of the son.

THAT HOUR

*You should write a poem for Nathaniel's Naming. But not
one of your usual ones.*

Pauline Sheard

In that hour after you were born,
I walked out in a new wool coat
too thin for the cold,
and surely that is why I trembled.

In that hour after you were born,
I was a ghost in the dark and silent town,
the frozen pavements narrow as tightropes,
and surely that is why I trod more lightly,
as if dancing.

In that hour after you were born,
I let the smoke of a dry tobacco
curl down a throat made raw by winter,
and surely that is why each breath I took
took out my heart.

In that hour after you were born,
I entertained a pre-dawn drunk
in an empty bus station.
He had no son.
And surely that is why I shared with him
the fragment that I knew.

In that hour after you were born,
I slumbered in a small, slow bus.
My eyelids fell,
and surely that is why the dawn that rose
around the sullen lump of Bosley Cloud
was like sunrise over Capri,
or new light falling
on the perfect stretch of Baltic shore.

In that hour after you were born,
I turned a key. And because a house
left vacant for the night is always strange
the space beyond the opening door
felt warmer, richer, changed.

NATHANIEL AT NEWBOROUGH

You were happy with the sand of the path,
fed handfuls to the spiny dune grass.
Laid flat. Made wing-shapes.
Chose three stones for later work.

Chivvied on, you broke into a bigger world,
a bigger sky and the shiny levels spread wide.
The far arms of the headlands held it and you.
A tideline of pebbles wobbled your ankles

and you giggled. You dabbled in a pool,
saw threadlike fish, the dead crab
with its boned white belly up,
the drifting *Ow!Ow!* jelly blob.

And this is the slow and ceaseless piston
of the sea, son. Watch it move, then let it take you
at your ankles, knees, then waist.
Fall, laugh, then stand again.
Fall, laugh, then stand again.

THE LAST POEM

The last poem was not wrought.
It was not inlaid. It was unveined.

It was not a mechanism, skeletal
or industrial. It was not set ticking

by the moving fingers of a craftsman
or soothed upwards into blossom.

And because it was never open,
the last poem did not click shut

with a pleasing sound, like a box
with a perfect hinge and a perfect catch.

It held no jewels.

The last poem was not luminous.
It did not vibrate. It evoked

not very much at all.

It sat fat and leaden in the hand, like that.
It curled the holder's fingers around it,

just so.

ACKNOWLEDGEMENTS

Acknowledgements are due to the editors of the following:

Keele Writing, London Review of Books, Mews Press, Mimesis